LOST!
Surviving in the Wilderness

Survivors: Ordinary People, Extaordinary Circumstances

An Enemy Within:
Overcoming Cancer and Other Life-Threatening Diseases

Danger in the Deep:
Surviving Shark Attacks

Gender Danger:
Survivors of Rape, Human Trafficking, and Honor Killings

In Defense of Our Country:
Survivors of Military Conflict

Lost!
Surviving in the Wilderness

Nature's Wrath:
Surviving Natural Disasters

Never Again:
Survivors of the Holocaust

Students in Danger:
Survivors of School Violence

Survival Skills:
How to Handle Life's Catastrophes

Those Who Remain:
What It Means to Be a Survivor

We Shall All Be Free:
Survivors of Racism

When Danger Hits Home:
Survivors of Domestic Violence

The World Gone Mad:
Surviving Acts of Terrorism

LOST!
Surviving in the Wilderness

Zachary Chastain

 Mason Crest Publishers

LOST! Surviving in the Wilderness

MASON CREST PUBLISHERS INC.
370 Reed Road
Broomall, Pennsylvania 19008
(866)MCP-BOOK (toll free)
www.masoncrest.com

Because the stories in this series are told by real people, in some cases names have been changed to protect the privacy of the individuals.

First Printing
9 8 7 6 5 4 3 2 1

ISBN 978-1-4222-0449-8 (series)
ISBN 978-1-4222-1462-6 (series) (pbk.)

Library of Congress Cataloging-in-Publication Data

Chastain, Zachary.
  Lost! : surviving in the wilderness / Zachary Chastain.
       p. cm.
  Includes bibliographical references and index.
  ISBN 978-1-4222-1466-4 (pbk.) — ISBN 978-1-4222-0453-5 (hardback)
  1. Resilience (Personality trait) 2. Survival after airplane accidents, shipwrecks, etc. 3. Survival. I. Title.
  BF698.35.R47C43 2009
  613.6'9—dc22
                                    2008044474

Design by MK Bassett-Harvey.
Produced by Harding House Publishing Service, Inc.
www.hardinghousepages.com
Cover design by Wendy Arakawa.
Printed in The Hashimite Kingdom of Jordan.

CONTENTS

Introduction

Each of us is confronted with challenges and hardships in our daily lives. Some of us, however, have faced extraordinary challenges and severe adversity. Those who have lived—and often thrived—through affliction, illness, pain, tragedy, cruelty, fear, and even near-death experiences are known as survivors. We have much to learn from survivors and much to admire.

Survivors fascinate us. Notice how many books, movies, and television shows focus on individuals facing—and overcoming—extreme situations. *Robinson Crusoe* is probably the earliest example of this, followed by books like the *Swiss Family Robinson*. Even the old comedy *Gilligan's Island* appealed to this fascination, and today we have everything from the Tom Hanks' movie *Castaway* to the hit reality show *Survivor* and the popular TV show *Lost*.

What is it about survivors that appeals so much to us? Perhaps it's the message of hope they give us. These people have endured extreme challenges—and they've overcome them. They're ordinary people who faced extraordinary situations. And if they can do it, just maybe we can too.

This message is an appropriate one for young adults. After all, adolescence is a time of daily challenges. Change is everywhere in their lives, demanding that they adapt and cope with a constantly shifting reality. Their bodies change in response to increasing levels of sex hormones; their thinking processes change as their brains develop, allowing them to think in more abstract ways; their social lives change as new people and peers become more important. Suddenly, they experience the burning need to form their own identities. At the same time, their emotions are labile and unpredictable. The people they were as children may seem to have disappeared beneath the onslaught of new emotions, thoughts, and sensations. Young adults have to deal with every single one of these changes, all at the same time. Like many of the survivors whose stories are told in this series, adolescents' reality is often a frightening, confusing, and unfamiliar place.

Young adults are in crises that are no less real simply because these are crises we all live through (and most of us survive!) Like all survivors, young adults emerge from their crises transformed; they are not the people they were before. Many of them bear scars they will carry with them for life—and yet these scars can be integrated into their new identities. Scars may even become sources of strength.

In this book series, young adults will have opportunities to learn from individuals faced with tremendous struggles. Each individual has her own story, her own set of circumstances and challenges, and her own way of coping and surviving. Whether facing cancer or abuse, terrorism or natural disaster, genocide or school violence, all the survivors who tell their stories in this series have found the ability and will to carry on despite the trauma. They cope, persevere, persist, and live on as a person changed forever by the ordeal and suffering they endured. They offer hope and wisdom to young adults: if these people can do it, so can they!

These books offer a broad perspective on life and its challenges. They will allow young readers to become more self-aware of the demanding and difficult situations in their own lives—while at the same time becoming more compassionate toward those who have gone through the unthinkable traumas that occur in our world.

— Andrew M. Kleiman, M.D.

Chapter One

WILDERNESS AND HUMAN LIFE

At some point in your life, you will come to the edge of what you know. For most of us, this happens over and over throughout our lives, in one way or another. We arrive outside the limits of our knowledge, our experience, and are forced to make a decision: How do I survive in this unknown place? It is an essential question, one that human beings have always asked. It speaks to the core of what it means to be a human creature, something that needs certain requirements in order to survive: food, water, shelter, and warmth.

NATURE'S ROLE IN OUR LIVES

Most people will agree that human beings came from the Earth. Many religions have creation stories in which a god creates humans out of the Earth's materials in order to interact with the created world. But what name do we give to this place we live, this dirt beneath our feet, sky above our heads, creatures living below, beside, and above us?

We call it nature. Nature is all around us. We are a part of nature. The very oxygen and carbon dioxide we breathe in and out is shared by trees, plants, other animals, and even other planets and stars. The more we discover about nature and its workings, the more we discover it to be a vast system of interconnected organisms. Each organism affects and is affected by other organisms, so that the disappearance of bees could disturb the growth of flowers, which could harm the health of certain crops that humans eat to survive. In nature, everything is connected.

But not everyone views nature this way. In fact, over the course of history, our attitude toward nature has continually changed. And as our attitude toward nature has changed, so has our attitude toward wilderness areas. We cannot talk about wilderness without talking about nature, of which wilderness is a part.

WHAT IS WILDERNESS?

The most basic definition of wilderness is land that is untamed by humans. Wilderness lands are usually treacherous to human health, such as climates of extreme cold, heat,

wetness, or dryness. Wilderness can also simply be land that has never been charted—those blank white spaces on a map.

In the earliest eras of human history, almost all land was uncharted by humans. Early humans had very little control over the land in which they lived. These people were **migratory**, moving in relatively small numbers from unknown place to unknown place in search of food. Probably about the time that they began to predict the weather

Nature is beautiful, but surviving in the wilderness can take skill.

migratory: wandering, moving from place to place, often with the seasons.

inseparable: impossible to separate; very closely connected.

Things in nature are interconnected and exist in a delicate balance.

patterns of one place, they'd run out of food and move on to another. To them, nature and wilderness were nearly **inseparable**. The natural world they existed in was a wild one. It was full of the dangerous and untamed.

It wasn't until people began settling in villages—growing their own food and raising animals—that the modern idea of wilderness really began to take shape. When societies develop, and civilizations emerge, lines get drawn and territory gets defined. The wilder-

The Meaning of "Wilderness" in the Thirteenth Century

People who study words tell us that the word "wilderness" was first written around 1200. It came from Old English words that meant "wild" + "animal" + "state of being." The Dutch and the Germans of the same period had similar words—*wildernis* and *wildnis*.

ness retreats beyond the well-tended fields. But nature does not. The early farmers knew that they could not separate themselves from the natural world.

Environmental scientists are only recently documenting what many farmers have learned from generations of experience and passed-on wisdom: we need the natural world. And while we may draw boundary lines on our maps and in our heads, nature does not. The farmer's field is not so different from the forest that surrounds it. When communities depend on land to put food on their plates, they tend to care about how that land is treated. Their survival depends on the Earth.

But as the years went by, technology advanced, and civilizations grew, things got more complicated. The gap widened between people's dinner plates and the soil that grew their food. As populations demanded more food, people began eating food from land where they no longer lived. Food might travel only a few miles—or it might travel thousands—but the ultimate effect is the same: people begin to ignore the importance of Nature, and wilderness seemed faraway and **irrelevant** to their lives. It became more important to dominate the land to bring about desired results than to listen to the Earth's natural cycles.

Today, land is still required to grow food, and wilderness is as important as ever if agriculture is to continue. But not everyone realizes that. More than ever before, we live in an industrial world. Some characteristics of industrial cultures are population move-

Nature is
necessary to
our survival.

One Man's Experience

Pinned down by a fallen boulder, climber and adventurer Aron Ralston thought about his coming death. After unsuccessfully struggling for days to escape, he had begun to accept that he would die alone in the wild. At first he was angry, but soon his anger turned into self-examination: he began to question his life-long hunger for near-death situations. As a mountain climber, he'd laughed in the face of death many times before. He developed a taste for long solo journeys into the wild. He enjoyed the age-old rivalry of "Man vs. Wild"—him against a mountain. As he hung in the ravine, waiting to die, Ralston wondered if his coming death was the unavoidable fate of continually pushing himself to the edge. After his rescue, he looked at his life in a very different way.

ment toward cities, **specialization** of skills and work, and an emphasis on machine labor.

In order for industrial societies to function, wilderness is contained and isolated. This is why wilderness "preserves" exist today. These are special places set apart from society where nature is allowed to carry on without human interference.

specialization: focusing on specific areas of knowledge or purposes, rather than on general ones.

WHAT DOES IT TAKE TO LIVE IN THE WILD?

The more people who live in urban and suburban communities, the fewer people who interact with nature on a daily basis. This means they no longer have the skills needed to even cope with the demands of living close to the Earth. Instead, specialized wilderness skills have developed along-side specialized wilderness spaces. So in the twentieth century a whole sector of the economy and society consists of people who buy and sell wilderness supplies and skills. Industrialized society provides specialized wilderness guides and experts who can take ordinary citizens into wilderness areas as part of vacations or team-building exercises. In many people's minds, the wilderness has become something like a park, a recreation area, rather than a foundation for our life, an essential piece of our Earth.

The change didn't happen over night, and it certainly hasn't been the same story in every part of the world. In fact, a few societies still force humans to submit to nature on a daily basis.

WHAT DOES THE WILDERNESS TEACH US?

Different people perceive nature differently. Some see in nature a total **indifference** to humans and their survival. They view nature with what they would call **rationality**, **objectively** and scientifically **quantifying** nature and finding it totally without affection (or any emotion at all) toward human beings. They argue that it is actually human beings

indifference: a lack of concern or interest.

rationality: being reasonable and practical.

objectively: in a way that considers actual existence and is not influenced by emotion or personal experience.

quantifying: determining the quantity of something; measuring and reducing a thing to scientific data.

who feel angry or loving toward wilderness, not the other way around. We are the change-ful ones, continually shaping and reshaping our opinion of the world. But nature, they would argue, never wavers. It is amoral, neither good nor evil.

Others feel differently. They see in nature the forms and impressions of a higher realm

The wilderness can be barren and beautiful.

City parks set
aside small
areas of nature,
although
they cannot
truly be called
wilderness.

of being. In nature, they believe, are the spirits and pathways to transcending normal human life. People who believe this usually find **solace** in nature. They want to be "in harmony" with its ways and find meaning in the acts of nature.

solace: comfort, consolation.

What's interesting is that most all perceptions of nature do not deny that the human experience in nature is that of a small being within a much larger one. For all that humans have tremendous technological powers, when we're stripped of these, we find ourselves naked and vulnerable to the blast of nature's fury. Especially in survival situations, human beings are pitted against towering forces. They have to come to terms with the scale of themselves within their surroundings. They are insignificant within the whirlwind of weather, terrain, and animal life.

And yet even in these extreme situations, where everything is stripped away from them, human beings have an amazing ability to survive. Cushioned by our modern world, we sometimes forget that we are also equipped with a powerful mind and body, both of which are capable of adapting to a vast **array** of circumstances. What other species besides humans has rocketed into outer space, climbed to the earth's highest places, and explored its deepest oceans and coldest terrains?

array: a large group or number of something.

Some people believe that confronting the wilderness allows us to become more fully

Animals do not see the boundaries between wilderness and civilization as humans do.

human. This is one reason why wilderness survival is attractive to so many. They are looking for a place to find out more about what it means to be human. They believe there is no better place to do so than in the wild, out beyond the edge of civilization.

It may very well be that a search for an inner "edge" is what drives so many towards wilderness in the twenty-first century. With so much of our experience tamed, many people are looking toward the Earth's remaining wildernesses for places to push themselves past the ordinary. The wild provides a chance to go into some unknown place within ourselves, a place where anything is possible.

Chapter Two
THE SCIENCE OF STAYING WARM

If you live in a part of the world where temperatures drop below freezing, you've probably experienced what it's like to be caught outside in the "bitter cold." There's a reason those words—"bitter" and "cold"—so often appear together. As soon as human beings understood the cycle of seasons, from spring to summer, fall to winter, they realized that winter was the most challenging season. Surviving this season required a good deal of preparation and a healthy respect for its dangers.

Humans are warm-blooded creatures. Warm-blooded creatures maintain thermal homeostasis, which means they keep their body temperatures as constant as possible. In some ways, everything we warm-blooded creatures do is related to this battle for our internal temperature.

The term "arctic" is given to the region around the Earth's North Pole, and the term "Antarctic" to the region around the Earth's South Pole.

HOW DOES YOUR BODY STAY WARM?

complex: made up of many parts; complicated.

Many of the body's methods of temperature control have something to do with what we call metabolism. Metabolism refers to an incredibly **complex** system of chemical reactions that occur in living organisms in order to support life. Digestion (a part of that process) is a heat-generating process—and food is the fuel the body burns to heat itself. Food gets turned into energy or stored as fat, which can later be broken down by other metabolic processes and turned into heat.

Muscular activity converts fats and sugars into heat; in other words, it speeds up the metabolic process. When you've been outside in the cold too long, and your teeth start chattering, that's actually your muscles

Cooling Systems

Anytime you eat, move, or sleep, your internal body temperature is subject to change, and your body must make adjustments accordingly. For example, intense exercise raises your body temperature and your body must sweat to cool you back down. Sweating uses evaporation to cool you down, since turning liquids (in this case, your sweat) into gases results in an overall heat loss. Other warm-blooded species, like dogs, have few or no sweat glands and must find other ways to cool themselves, such as panting with their tongues hanging out.

activating. It's a reflex that helps your body generate heat.

Your body's most important heat-conserving method, however, is insulation. Insulation can come in many forms. The natural forms are fat and fur, but most humans don't have enough of these to do them much good when facing extreme cold. For humans in the wilderness, insulation most often looks like socks, boots, thermal underwear, and nylon jackets—in other words, clothing. The naked human body is not naturally equipped for survival in the cold, so we must use other means to keep heat. But most other warm-blooded creatures rely on fur, skin, or blubber to keep heat trapped inside their bodies.

THE INUIT

When you think about survival in the world's coldest environments, you probably don't realize that there are actually people who've chosen to live in these places for thousands of years. Languages and culture vary among the peoples of these arctic regions, but what most have in common is skill in adapting to a harsh environment.

How do they do it? How do they survive with so little of the technology of their southern neighbors? For the Inuit, the lands they inhabit are no wilderness. But that doesn't mean you and I would find them any less dangerous or wild; these peoples have totally

The Inuit are, in fact, the creators of the "qajaq," or what Europeans later called a kayak. This light-weight water craft was built out of seal skins and timber and could easily be righted if flipped upside down.

Did You Know?

Blubber is a thick layer of fat found under the skin of many warm-blooded creatures. It is an excellent insulator. Whales and many seals have particularly high levels of fat stored as blubber. Unlike sea otters and other furred creatures, animals with blubber are able to swim much deeper and remain longer in extremely cold water because of their blubber. Some whales can live in waters with temperatures as low as –40 degrees Fahrenheit (that's also –40 Celsius).

In the far north, within the arctic rim, native peoples (often called Inuit) have long hunted whales for their energy rich blubber. These peoples are able to survive such extreme climates in large part because blubber is such an excellent source of both energy and nutrients. You'd think that such a high-fat diet might not be good for them, but that's not the case. So healthy is their traditional blubber diet that, on average, a seventy-year-old Inuit has arteries as healthy as those of a 20-year-old European.

The Inuit followed the migrations of the caribou herds and other arctic animals.

adapted their lifestyles to the land. They know how to live with the cold.

For most of Inuit history, these peoples have been **nomadic**, following land animals, birds, fish, and sea mammals in order to survive. They developed fine-tuned techniques that used all available resources to the fullest extent. These peoples have learned to do much with what we might see as very little. Those who need to learn about

nomadic: having no fixed home, but instead wandering from place to place.

surviving in the arctic often turn to the Inuit for lessons.

SURVIVING THREE DAYS IN THE ARCTIC

Gary Benton was a brand new officer when he got the call telling him he'd be required to take part in an "Arctic Survival Course" as part of his service in the United States Air Force. He did so willingly, but with a sense of dread (along with most of his fellow airmen). In his account of that first day, Benton remembers stepping out of the classroom and into the frigid air. The training sergeant informed his men that the temperature was –20 degrees Fahrenheit that day (–28.9 Celsius), and would drop well below that come nightfall.

Benton looked around at his fellow students. Although they, like him, had spent the past few weeks training for precisely this moment, they all looked terrified. Benton knew he looked just as scared. Now that he was outside, and the actual cold was pressing in on him, he couldn't imagine lasting more than a few hours, let alone three days, in such weather.

Benton began reminding himself of all the safety nets in place around him: each airman would go into the wild with a buddy nearby, and buddies could assist one another in an emergency. The sergeants carried radios in case anyone needed medical attention. This was certainly not a real-life survival situation,

In many parts of the world, wilderness survival means dealing with snow, ice, and extremely cold temperatures.

Wearing warm clothes means your body has to use less energy to survive cold temperatures.

but it was about as close to one as you could get without actually crashing a plane. It was enough to scare Benton. His training told him, however, that fear is only normal in wilderness survival situations, and that the proper response is to get busy. Idleness only fuels a sense of helplessness.

So once out in the cold, Gary Benton got to work. His first task: to build a fire. Lucky for the survival students, the training facility was south of the latitude north of which no trees can grow, so firewood was available. If the exercise had been conducted a few hundred miles farther north, the trainees would have had to make do without a fire.

Benton began looking for kindling, the smallest dry wood he could find for his fire—usually dead twigs at the base of a tree. Because there were pine trees near his campsite, he had access to pine pitch, a naturally flammable substance that helps start fires. Pitch is usually a light orange color, and can be collected in globs and added to kindling. Next it was time to gather larger pieces of wood for the fire, which Benton did until he had enough for the rest of the day.

He was careful not to spend more time than necessary building his fire, as he'd actually be spending most of the next three days inside his shelter, and he needed to start working on it before nightfall. This fire's purpose would mostly be to keep him warm while he spent the rest of his time constructing a shelter.

Of course Benton wouldn't have been able to start his fire if he didn't have a small but essential survival kit along with him. It consisted merely of a small plastic baggy, inside which he kept dryer lint, steel, and flint. The kit was small enough to fit inside a wallet or pocket if need be. Once the delicate fibers of the lint were lit, Benton added first small kindling, then larger and larger pieces of wood until the fire was **self-sustaining**. With this accomplished, he could move on to the shelter.

self-sustaining: able to provide for one's own needs without help from outside sources.

hypothermia:
an abnormally
low body
temperature,
often caused
by exposure to
cold over a long
period of time.

Knowing how
to build a fire in
the wild can be
very useful.

Strangely enough, one of the first things Benton did was take off his parka. He did this to avoid sweating. Sweating in arctic temperatures can lead to chilling and possibly **hypothermia**, and should be avoided at all costs. His next step was to dig a trench into the snow about three feet wide, three feet deep, and seven feet long. Nick Middleton, author of the survival book *Extremes*, calls such snow trenches "ice coffins." Of course, if all goes according to plan, this trench should be just the opposite of a coffin, but you get the idea: this is a very small liv-

ing space. You want it to hold your body heat as tightly as possible. Once the trench was made, Benton lined the floor of his shelter with pine boughs from nearby trees. Other types of trees can be used for flooring, just so long as they adequately guard against the cold snow beneath your shelter. Benton piled his pine boughs a little over a foot thick.

With this done, Benton put his gear in the shelter up against the far wall, away from where the entrance would soon be. Then he began to gather logs for the roof. He piled the logs beside the trench, not wanting to make more trips into the woods once he'd begun work. Starting at the end opposite his entrance, he laid logs and limbs over the open trench until he had it covered almost entirely, leaving only a small opening big enough for his body. An entrance should be fitted to body size so that as little heat as possible is lost. Benton then inspected the edges of the roof to be sure each log overlapped the side of his trench by about a foot on each side. These logs needed to bear the weight of the rest of the roof, which Benton then began. He placed pine boughs atop the roof for needed insulation. Because Benton's exercise **simulated** a plane-crash situation, he had been given a parachute. This valuable resource he used as a tarp stretched over the pine boughs, and then he covered the chute with a layer of snow. The roof was complete.

At this point, Benton took a break. He had a container with him, which he filled with

simulated:
created the appearance or experience of.

Snow can
be used as
insulation from
the colder air
and wind.

snow and then boiled over the fire for clean water. Staying **hydrated** and not sweating is extremely important in cold temperatures, so taking a break to drink water and cool down is a good idea.

hydrated: supplied with water.

But Benton's survival job was not complete. He still had two important tasks to do before his shelter was ready for the coming night. He crawled inside his shelter for the first time and poked a hole about three inches in diameter in the top of his shelter. This hole would allow for ventilation inside the shelter, a much needed addition if he wanted to breathe fresh air and avoid carbon monoxide poisoning. Also, he had brought along a small candle that he would burn inside his shelter, and that too would use up precious oxygen. His final step was to construct a door for his shelter. He cut a piece of his parachute off and filled it with snow, then tied it off to form a sack about the size of his shelter's entrance. By rolling this sack into place, he was able to seal off his shelter.

That evening, Benton's training sergeant came to check on him and examine his shelter. Benton was quite proud of what he'd done and expected a compliment. The straight-faced sergeant only said, "Not bad. Not good either. We will see tonight if it is good enough." Fortunately, the next three days proved that it was good enough, and although Benton still had to fight boredom, hunger, and discomfort, he successfully completed his arctic survival training.

STORMS

Storms are particularly hazardous to you in extreme-cold survival situations. This is why the concept of shelter is emphasized so heavily in cold-weather survival guides. Above all else, you have to be prepared for that whiteout or blizzard that could trap you in one place for days. Even with the best equipment and with plenty of preparation, no one is ever totally safe from unexpected acts of nature. Storms prove this point well.

Blizzards and whiteouts can be dangerous, even when civilization is not far away.

A SKIING TRIP GONE WRONG

On December 19, 1998, Nick Williams decided to catch a few hours of skiing at Squaw Valley in California. It was a standard ski trip for fifty-one-year-old Williams—just a few hours of relaxation and alone time, maybe some light exercise at most. The day was clear, and the weather forecast called for temperatures in the thirties (around 0 Celsius), with light snow. Williams figured his Dallas Cowboy's jacket was all he needed for protection.

He was going up the chair lift for his fourth run when the blizzard hit, whiting out the entire slope. Instead of waiting the storm out or taking the lift back down, Williams decided to take matters into his own hands. He wanted to get back to the lodge quickly. Checking his basic lodge-issued map of the mountain, he realized he could be back at the lodge in a few minutes if he cut through a nearby tree line.

If only it were so easy. Williams soon found himself staring down a 500-foot cliff with a valley below. He was lost and stranded in a blizzard with no food, water, cold-weather clothing, or matches. For hours he struggled against the storm, pushing himself uphill and then skiing back down, looking for a way to retrace his already snow-covered tracks. He was fighting a losing battle, and night was falling fast. After a while he ditched his skis, thinking there was little else he could do on them.

Darkness brought the coldest temperatures yet, and still it kept snowing. Williams melted snow in his mouth for water and did calisthenics—jumping, stretching, kicking—to keep himself warm. All night he struggled to stay awake in the numbing cold.

The blizzard continued the next day, and soon he was working against snow that came up to his thighs. Disaster finally struck when he fell through ice over a snow-covered stream, soaking his feet inside his boots. In a race against time, Williams tried to start a fire. He gathered wood against a granite stone and struck his ski pole against it until it finally broke. No sparks. Nothing. Later he would learn that had he been able to start a fire and thaw his feet, he would have lost both of them to amputation.

The second night came on harder than the first, with temperatures recorded at a nearby station at 19 degrees below zero (–28 Celsius). With wind chill accounted for, Williams probably suffered through temps as low as 50 below zero that night (–45 Celsius). Hypothermia had taken control of his body, causing incontrollable shaking and loss of mental ability. Throughout it all he had the will to survive, however; he kept praying and thinking of his family. His wife and son were on vacation in Florida, and they would be expecting him to join them next week. . . .

What eventually saved Williams' life was his work life. When he missed appointments the next day, business associates contacted

Someone Who *Didn't* Survive

Robert Falcon Scott was a British explorer of Antarctica who died because of a storm. In 1912, he and his men died miles away from their destination. His journals and papers are compiled in *Scott's Last Expedition*, and the following is one of his last journal entries on a failed mission. Scott and his men came head to head with a massive storm that kept them from making the final miles to safety. This entry was written just prior to his death.

> Our wreck is certainly due to this sudden advent of severe weather, which does not seem to have any satisfactory cause. I do not think human beings ever came through such a month as we have come through, and we should have got through in spite of the weather but for the sickening of a second companion, Captain Oates, and a shortage of fuel in our depots for which I cannot account, and finally, but for the storm which has fallen on us within 11 miles of the depot at which we hoped to secure out final supplies. Surely misfortune could scarcely have exceeded this last blow… We took risks, we knew we took them; things have come out against us, and therefore we have no cause for complaint, but bow to the will of Providence, determined still to do our best to the last…
>
> Had we lived, I should have had a tale to tell of the hardihood, endurance, and courage of my companions which would have stirred the heart of every Englishman. These rough notes and our dead must tell the tale.

his wife, who immediately knew something was wrong. Authorities informed her that no one could survive two nights in a blizzard, especially dressed as lightly as William was. She was told to make funeral arrangements.

Squaw Valley, California, where Nick Williams survived three days outside in a blizzard.

But on the third day the storm cleared. Williams found his way into direct sunlight and warmed himself. At about noon, he heard snowmobiles and shortly after he was spotted. A helicopter lifted him out. He lost all his toes but three. But he survived.

HYPOTHERMIA

Hypothermia is a condition in which the body's temperature falls into a below-average range and cannot recover without heat from an outside source. If you don't get that outside heat soon, you will die. It is the great enemy of winter weather travelers, and a constant threat to survivors of the northern- and southernmost wildernesses.

Hypothermia can occur over the course of many hours, as you trudge through waist-high snow and lose heat by the mile, or it can occur in a matter of seconds, as you plunge through ice into water so cold you'll be dead in minutes if you don't escape. Hypothermia is **accelerated** when combined with factors of dehydration and extreme physical stress. Dehydration weakens your ability to circulate blood (heat), and physical stress takes away valuable energy needed to maintain your internal temp of 98.6 degrees Fahrenheit (37 Celsius).

accelerated: speeded up.

You've probably seen films or read stories where someone breaks through the thin ice of a pond or lake, then is pulled to safety, only to have their clothes stripped off and a fire started for them. This is actually a pretty accurate picture of what it takes to save someone who is hypothermic. You see, just insulating the body (wrapping it in warm blankets, for instance) will not save someone from hypothermia. The heat loss damage has already been done—this person needs to regain that heat in order to survive.

HOW DO YOU IDENTIFY HYPOTHERMIA?

extremities: hands and feet and the ends of the arms and legs; the parts of the body furthest from the torso.

Your body's primary goal is to protect its vital organs. This means your torso and brain are a much higher priority than your **extremities**. If you begin losing feeling in your fingers, toes, legs, and arms, this is a result of a self-protective process called "shunting," where your body slows circulation to these parts in order to save heat for the core. Most of us have had a mild taste of this in the form of cold toes or fingers, perhaps a red nose and ears, but few have experienced it in its most extreme. In hypothermia cases, this extreme is an unmistakable loss of sensation in all one's limbs.

Another telltale sign of hypothermia is shivering. Of course, this too is an experience most have had. But again, hypothermic shaking is severe and totally involuntary, and is a sure sign that worse things are on their way. In fact, once a hypothermic person stops shaking, this means he has progressed one step closer to collapse. At 95 to

After prolonged exposure to extremely cold temperatures, move quickly to prevent hypothermia.

96 degrees (about 35 Celsius), shaking is so violent that speech and coordination are difficult, and the person has a hard time making decisions. But once that temperature drops below 90 degrees (32 Celsius), the shivering will very suddenly stop. The person may be able to still control his body, but his mind is beginning to suffer; **hallucinations** as well as muscle spasms and **panic** are a symptom of this stage of hypothermia. Once body temperature goes below 86 degrees (30 Celsius), the person will lose consciousness and all body functions will slow to a crawl. If he

hallucinations: experiences affecting any of the senses and accompanied by a sense of reality, but without an external source.

panic: overwhelming terror.

plummets another 8 degrees to 78 (25.5 Celsius), death is usually not far away.

TREATING HYPOTHERMIA

If someone is in the advanced stages of hypothermia, you must get them to a medical facility if at all possible. If this is a wilderness survival situation, however, the following two steps must be taken:

1. Stop further heat loss.
2. Add warmth safely to reverse the hypothermic process.

Stopping Heat Loss

Evaporation is one way your body can lose heat. Evaporation is why you must strip someone with hypothermia of any wet clothes. Simply putting her by a blazing fire will not do the trick. You must take whatever wet clothes she has on and replace them with dry ones; sometimes no clothes are better than wet ones.

Convection, the movement of air, is another heat-loss danger. Getting out of the wind is a sure way to avoid heat loss of this kind. Make sure you get yourself or your friend out of the breeze.

Radiation is probably the most common cause of heat-loss in hypothermia victims. Your body radiates heat unless insulated with clothing or blankets.

Conduction is the final heat-loss path, usually occurring if a hypothermic person sits on cold snow or a seat colder than their body. Any object that might be colder than the hypothermic person should be removed from contact with her body.

Adding Warmth

Once you've done all you can to stop heat-loss, it's time to start carefully adding warmth. That word "carefully" is extremely important here. Impatience and ignorance can be fatal. Before you begin, establish what stage of hypothermia the person is in. If he is talking and fairly mobile, just give him hot liquids and stop further heat loss with blankets or a sleeping bag. But if he is unconscious or far advanced in the stages, more drastic action may be needed. Take it slow. A person with hypothermia in this stage is in an extremely fragile state of life. Any trigger—like too much heat at once—could cause **cardiac failure**.

So go very slowly, and start at the core, not the extremities. Remember, the body shut down the extremities for a reason. Blood in these regions will be sluggish and colder than blood in the core, so focus your attention on heating the core and allowing the core to heat the rest of the body. The core holds all the body's most vital organs. If cold blood from the extremities was to suddenly flood the core, it could cause a temperature loss and ultimately cardiac failure.

A healthy human body is an ideal warmer for the person with hypothermia. Two bodies

cardiac failure: a condition in which the heart can no longer pump enough blood to meet the body's needs.

pressed against one another allows the colder body to heat slowly but gradually, without the risk of heart failure. In medical facilities, often the person with hypothermia is heated only one degree per hour. Heat packs are placed on areas of the core with high **circulation**—along the neck, in the armpits, and over the kidneys.

circulation: the movement of blood through the blood vessels of the body, pumped by the heart.

FROSTBITE

First off, if you are treating yourself or someone else for frostbite, then chances are you have a case of hypothermia to attend to as well. Be sure to treat the hypothermia first, as it is the cause of any frostbite you may sustain.

Frostbite is a symptom of what we called the "shunting process"—closing off circulation to the extremities to provide warmth for the core. Basically, this shutting down results in the slow but sure death of the skin cells in the extremities. We call this frostbite. It is the result of flesh cells freezing. They expand, rupture, and eventually are destroyed by the cold. Frostbite is similar to burns in that it is measured by how deep the freeze has gone—the deeper the cells are frozen, the worse the damage will be. More minor frostbite injuries appear white or grayish, and the victim usually has pain or some sensation left in that region of his body. Deeper frostbite burns are hard, white, and lack any feeling. In these cases, there is a further risk of gangrene, which is the rotting of dead cells. Gangrene can lead to infection and death.

This is why it is so important to treat frostbite properly. If not done correctly, infection can set it and the person can die from a very treatable condition. When treating frostbite, your first consideration should be preventing the damaged area from further heat loss. Keep the area warm and clean. Remove any cold or wet clothing and replace it with sterile, warm wrapping. Do not rub the frostbitten area. Rubbing does not effectively transfer heat deep into the skin, but only further damages the frozen cells.

Do not warm any frostbitten areas that you think may be frozen again. Many people have caused themselves greater injury by heating frostbitten feet by a fire, only to refreeze them on the next leg of their journey. This freeze-thaw-freeze-thaw process is extremely harmful to the cells, and can lead to gangrene and possibly the need for amputation. If you heat up a frostbitten area, plan on keeping it warm.

Do not use heat sources that are too extreme. A blazing fire is not ideal, but works if you stand far enough away. The problem is that without sensation in the damaged area, it's impossible to tell if you are doing further damage by scorching already fragile cells. Use lukewarm to hot water to soak the frostbitten areas. This is the surest way to slowly and safely reheat yourself. It can be an extremely painful process. As the feeling

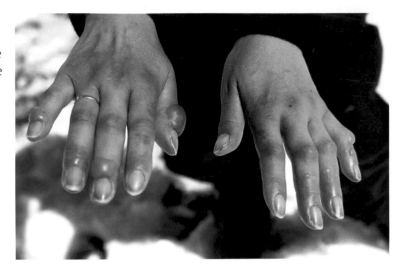

The woman in this picture lost the tips of three fingers from the frostbite on her hands.

comes back into your hands or feet, so does the pain of broken cells.

Remember, thawing the cells is a very dangerous process, and not recommended unless absolutely necessary. Many people have survived in the wild walking on frostbitten feet, using frostbitten hands. Of course, it's not ideal, but a few hours walk on frostbitten feet to a medical facility could be much safer than trying to thaw out in the wild.

THE LESSONS OF EXTREME COLD

The specific techniques we've discussed can help you survive a situation where you are stranded in an environment of extreme cold. Knowledge is an important tool for survival.

Ultimately, though, experts agree that survival is about more than knowledge, and it's also about more than tools and resources. Survival depends on what's inside of you. Whether you're facing extreme cold—or some other life-and-death situation, like cancer or war—your determination, as well as the depth of your connection to life, will be the largest factor in your survival.

According to Laurence Gonzales, author of *Deep Survival: Who Lives, Who Dies, and Why*, "Survivors discover a deep spiritual relationship to the world." Another author, Viktor Frankl, a survivor of the Holocaust, wrote of what he did to inspire others to survive the atrocities of the concentration camps:

> It was a question of getting them to realize that life was still expecting something from them; something in the future was expected of them. We found, in fact, that for the one it was his child whom he adored and who was waiting for him in a foreign country. For the other it was a thing, not a person. This man was a scientist and had written a series of books that still needed to be finished. His work could not be done by anyone else, any more than another person could ever take the place of the father in his child's affections.

No matter what the odds, people who are deeply connected to their families, their friends, and the activities in their lives—as Nick Williams was—make better survivors.

Chapter Three

LOST
IN THE
MOUNTAINS

You might have heard of Aron Ralston, and if you have, you likely know him only as "the guy who cut his arm off to survive." This is true. In May 2003, Aron Ralston's right arm was pinned beneath a boulder for five days before he amputated it with his pocketknife. But there is more to the story.

Ralston was no stranger to climbing. In fact, in 2002 he quit his job in order to climb all of Colorado's "fourteeners," the mountains over 14,000 feet high. Ralston was twenty-seven years old, very physically fit, and an experienced climber—but he made a terrible mistake before ever stepping foot in Utah's Blue John Canyon. He had broken the first rule of solo climbing and outdoor exploration: always tell someone where you're going.

This particular trip was a detour of sorts for Ralston, not even a climbing expedition, but

Blue John Canyon, Utah, where Aron Ralston's hand was trapped under a boulder.

rather what is called a "canyoneering" trip. Canyoneering is climbing up and down the deep cracks and crevasses carved into rock canyons. Not expecting to be gone long or encounter the dangers of a steep mountain slope, Ralston went alone and without leaving information about his whereabouts or when he should be expected to return.

It happened while he was descending into a slot canyon. An 800-pound boulder (363 kg) tumbled down, trapping his right hand and wrist. He tried everything, but at first he wasn't too worried. After all, this same scenario threatens mountain climbers all the time. Using his climbing equipment to give him leverage, he pushed and he pulled, but nothing budged the massive stone.

Before long, even the pain was gone; numbness had set in. Ralston knew his options were dwindling. Because of the **remoteness** of his location, another canyoneer was unlikely to find him until the following weekend. Waiting for help would likely kill him. Moving the rock has also proven impossible. With little else left to do, Ralston turned his attention to a last resort: amputation.

But how? He needed two vital tools: something sharp enough to do the job, and a **tourniquet** to stop the bleeding. At this point, however, amputation was really only a mental exercise, something to occupy his mind, not an option he was seriously considering. He didn't believe the pocketknife he had with him would be big enough to sever his wrist. Besides, the thought of amputating his own arm horrified him. As the thought became less easy to avoid, he wrote in his book, it actually made him vomit.

Ralston had brought with him on this trek a small video camera. About a day and half into the ordeal, he took it out of his bag and turned it on. He talked through the story of the past day and a half, enjoying the **illusion** that he was no longer quite so alone. Addressing

remoteness: being isolated, far away, separated by a great distance.

tourniquet: something used to stop bleeding by compressing the blood vessels, generally a bandage tightened by twisting.

illusion: a false and deceiving perception of reality.

the camera, he took stock of his physical health. And finally, he estimated how much longer he had to live and said his good-byes in case he didn't survive.

In his book, *Between a Rock and a Hard Place*, Ralston recorded these video confessions:

> So, either somebody notices I'm missing because I don't show up at the house for the party on Monday night or I don't show up for work on Tuesday, but they don't really know more than I went to Utah. I think maybe my truck will be found. I think it will be Wednesday, Thursday, at the earliest when someone figures out where I might be, what I've done, and gets to me. That's at least three days from now. Judging by my **degradation** in the last twenty-four hours, I'll be surprised if I make it to Tuesday. I'm sorry. Mom, Dad, I love you. Sonja, I love you. You guys make me proud. I don't know what it is about me that's brought me to this. But this is . . . what I've been after. I go out looking for adventure and risk so I can feel alive. But I got by myself and don't tell someone where I'm going, that's just dumb. If someone knew, if I'd have been with someone else, there would probably already be help on the way. Even if I'd just talked to a ranger or left a note on my truck. Dumb, dumb, dumb.

degradation: a wearing and breaking down into a lower state.

Things can go wrong even for experienced climbers, like the man here or like Aron Ralston.

Things got worse for Ralston. No help came. What little water and food he had brought with him was used up. He began saving his urine in his CamelPak (a hiker's water pack), which filtered some of the salt and sediment and made it drinkable.

On the fifth day, Ralston began to fully accept death. He even **inscribed** the words "RIP OCT 75 ARON APR 03" into the rock

inscribed: marked or wrote letters or symbols on a surface.

wall. He was certain this was the day of his death.

Ralston was truly desperate now. A day earlier, he had begun cutting through his forearm with the shorter of two pocket-knives. He had been stopped, as he'd worried he would, by his forearm bones. But then he had a revelation: what if he swung his body left and right, turning the arm like a two-by-four board in a vise? The motion worked. Ralston was able to snap both his bones and then continue sawing through his bloody wrist. When he got to the tougher tendons, he switched to the pliers on his pocket tool and tore the tendons that way. It was a brutal process, but he managed to keep his cool throughout. Luckily, most of the feeling in that part of his arm was gone, leaving only a few nerve bundles to cause him pain.

When he finally accomplished the task, and his body slumped to the ground, he could hardly believe it. He gathered his things, and even took the time to take two digital photographs of his severed hand still caught between the rocks. He walked miles into the canyon where he was met by a family of three who gave him the only food they had—two Oreo cookies—and a liter of water.

Ralston had survived.

TRAPPED IN THE ANDES

On October 13, 1972, a group of forty-five Uruguayans found themselves trapped in mountain terrain. Their situation was vastly different from Aron Ralston's. They were not alone, and most of the survivors had full use of their bodies. But they were effectively just as trapped as Aron Ralston was—pinned down not by a rock but by harsh weather.

Uruguayan Air Force Flight 571 was an airline flight carrying these forty-five people from Montevideo, Uruguay, to Santiago, Chile. On board was a rugby team from Stella Maris College, and with them their friends and family. Because of a mountain storm, the plane had to stop overnight in the town of Mendoza, and when they departed the next day for their destination, disaster struck. The plane was cruising far too low to be passing over the Andes mountain range, which has many high-altitude peaks, but the pilots seemed to be unaware of this and thought

The Andes Mountains, where the Uruguayan flight crashed.

they were passing through a much safer "pass" that was farther south. The pilots had entered thick clouds and had to rely on estimated time to know when to make the turn toward the mountains. They didn't anticipate the strong headwinds that had slowed them down, and they took the turn too early—straight into the heart of the Andes.

The plane briefly emerged from the cloud cover seconds before the crash, giving pilot and passengers alike time to shriek in terror as they watched their plane speed toward an oncoming mountain. With no time to maneuver, the plane's right wing was clipped off by a mountain peak and then tore through the tail end of the plane, ripping it completely off the plane's body. A few passengers were sucked out the now-open rear; then the right wing too was clipped off by another peak, and the body of the plane plummeted to a

The wreckage of Uruguayan Air Force Flight 571 and the survivors at the time of rescue.

snowy bank, sliding hundreds of feet before coming to a halt.

Of the forty-five people on board, twelve died in the crash or soon after, five died by next morning, and one died eight days later of injuries from the crash. The remaining twenty-seven survivors now had to face the treacherous mountain terrain along with fiercely cold temperatures and little resources. The survivors lacked just about everything necessary for survival in the mountains. Most wore only light jackets or suit coats, and no one had suitable footwear for the snow. Additionally, some had broken bones that needed splints. Two freshman medical students who had survived were able to create makeshift splints built from parts of the shattered aircraft.

What remained on the aircraft was, in general, very little: a few chocolate bars, other assorted snacks, and several bottles of wine. One of the survivors, Fito Strauch, was an inventor who was able to temporarily solve the water shortage by creating melting containers from metal on the airplane seats. These containers were filled with snow and placed on top of the plane. The snow melted and then dripped down into wine bottles.

Back in civilization, search parties from three countries began looking for the missing plane. Unfortunately, there was a significant problem: the plane was white, just about as white as the snow it was nestled into, and impossible to see from the sky. The search was cancelled after eight days. The passengers were assumed dead.

But they were very much alive. In fact, they were listening to the news of their crash on a small transistor radio they had found in the plane's cabin. The radio was incapable of sending messages, but it could receive radio waves. Eleven days after the crash, two survivors were listening in when they heard news that the search had been called off.

The moment was both emotionally crushing—and at the same time, an important turning point in the survivors' resolve. On the one hand, they were now completely on their own, without hope of outside rescue—but on the other, they now knew what to expect, and could prepare accordingly. They knew they could not sit **passively**, waiting for rescue.

passively:
without action
or resistance.

One of the survivors, a young man named Gustavo Nicolich, came out of the plane and addressed the depressed crowd of survivors. He asked if they had heard the good news—that they would not be rescued. They asked him how that could possibly be good news. "Because it means," he answered, "that we're going to get out of here on our own." This was an inspiration to the rest, who now needed courage and hope more than ever.

In the Southern Hemisphere, spring was on its way. The chosen leader of the survivors, Roberto Canessa, insisted that any expedition to the west to find a Chilean village must wait for warmer weather. A month passed, and before the survivors could make a difficult decision about how to find help, they had to make a more pressing decision: what to eat. Everyone knew that eating the dead passengers was an option, but of course the idea was gruesome to all. The dead were friends and family of the survivors. But something must be done, and finally a few began the horrific task of cutting flesh from the dead.

Meanwhile, a group of three healthy young men were being prepared for the dangerous trek into the mountains. They were fed the best rations and excused from the daily labor that the survivors did to maintain water and warmth. When these men were strong enough, they set out east, since they weren't able to go immediately west because a mountain blocked their way.

A short way into their journey, the men realized it would be nearly impossible to survive the cold nights without some form of shelter. Although during the days the temperature was now routinely above freezing, the nights were well below and deadly. So the men returned to the camp and began to work on sewing a giant sleeping bag from the plane's seating material. This enormous quilt would hold all three men, allowing them to use each other's heat and survive the cold nights.

On December 12, 1972, two months after the crash, the three men embarked again, this time heading west, up and over the mountain.

Nando Parrado
(in the center)
after his rescue.

They were determined to not stop until they found help. Of the three men, Nando Parrado reached the peak first, and when he did, he looked west over a seemingly endless stretch of mountains. He was determined not to let his spirits sink, however, as he saw in the distance what looked like green land.

The men hiked for several more days, finally reaching the end of the snow line. For the first time in months the three of them stood on black and green earth, instead of white snow. One of the men was Canessa, who thought he noticed what looked like a man on a horse across the river. Since his eyesight was poor and he thought it might be a trick of his imagination, he sent Parrado down to the river to check. Parrado confirmed that what they saw was not one man, but in fact three, and began shouting and waving his arms to signal that they needed help. The men indicated that they would bring help tomorrow.

Early the next day the men were brought across the river, then given access to rescue teams. They guided helicopter rescue teams to where the rest of the survivors were located, and all were eventually brought to nearby hospitals, where they were treated for **altitude sickness**, dehydration, frostbite, broken bones, **scurvy**, and **malnutrition**.

They had done things they had never thought possible, including eating human flesh. But they had survived.

TRAPPED IN THE GULLY

Malaysia's eastern island, Borneo, is the third largest island in the world. Borneo is home to thick rain forests and towering mountains. One particularly impressive peak that northern Borneo boasts is called Mount Kinabalu, and within its slopes lies Low's Gully. A gully is simply the name given to any deep ravine or cut in the earth, usually made by some movement of water—a river or waterfall, for instance. In the case of Low's Gully, three different waterfalls flow down into the gully's bottom and accumulate in a few small ponds. The walls of the gully are both rocky and steep, many of them almost entirely vertical, making the gully difficult and dangerous to get into.

To some, however, this is but another of nature's welcome challenges. A British army

altitude sickness: a condition caused by low air pressure, usually experienced at very high altitudes. It is characterized by headache, dizziness, shortness of breath, nausea, and swelling, and can be life threatening if untreated.

scurvy: a disease caused by a lack of vitamin C, characterized by bleeding gums and fatigue.

malnutrition: lack of sufficient nutrition.

The view from
the top of
Mt. Kinabalu,
Borneo.

training expedition under the command of
Lieutenant-Colonel Robert Neill accepted
Low's Gully's challenge. The ten-member
team had climbed Kinabalu and spent a few
days learning mountain survival skills before
descending into the gully.

In 1851, Sir Hugh Low, a British Colonial
Secretary, set out to explore Mount Kinabalu
with a traveling party of about forty men.

Low discovered that on the slope was what he called "a circular amphitheatre" in which he could not find an end. In other words, he and his men had stumbled upon a massive gully. Many of the men with Low were native to the island, and they told him of legends surrounding the mountain and this very gully. The legends spoke of a wronged dragon that lived deep in this "cave" (gully) in order to guard a huge jewel. The native men said that explorers had tried to steal the dragon's jewel, and as a result it had cursed this mountain and any who attempted to conquer it.

But the ten men descending the gully on February 22, 1994, cared little about the legend. They were looking for exercise and adventure, not precious stones. When the team began the descent, they broke into two smaller teams of five, led by Neill and another officer, Private Mayfield, who was the most experienced climber in the group. Unfortunately, because of bad communication and lesser climbing experience, Neill and his team soon fell well behind Mayfield's crew.

Neill was worried from the beginning about the rate of progress they were making down the slope, and by day six of the descent his fears were confirmed: they had completely lost contact with Mayfield's team. They emerged from a wooded portion of the slope onto a granite surface, and for the first time were able to look straight to the bottom of the gully. Mayfield's crew was nowhere to be seen. Where had they gone? The slope was steep enough that Neill was forced to question whether the other team had attempted it at all. After **assessing** the situation, Neill decided they had most likely continued downward. He then decided his team's only choice was to follow after them.

This proved a more difficult task than expected. Without Mayfield, Neill's team **abseiled** down the slope only a few dozen feet at a time, and to complicate things even further, the weather turned foul, and rain began to fall. The climbers now risked further injury on a slick surface. By day 10 the slope gave way to yet another vertical drop. In Neill's own words: "We were looking at air." Rations were running low, and things were not looking good.

At this point the five-man team consisted of two British officers, Neill and his second-in-command Ron Foster, and three Hong Kong soldiers. Neill decided it was best to halt all operations; the rest of the crew were relieved to hear this decision. After some thought, it was decided they should attempt to retreat back up the gully. But this proved impossible. Rain was falling hard and the climbers began looking desperately for shelter. One of the men, Kevin Cheung, found a cave.

At first, the men were delighted to find shelter from the rain. Little did they know, they would come to know this cave much more intimately than they ever imagined. It

assessing:
sizing up; determining the significance or importance of.

abseiled:
rappelled.

would form a crude base camp for the next three weeks. In his book *Survival*, Anthony Masters recounts the journal entries of both Foster and Neill. Foster gives the following reasons for remaining in the cave:

- Water too dangerous to carry on.
- Hong Kong soldiers need rest.
- Several minor injuries.
- Any escape must be planned properly in view of our failed attempt yesterday.
- Conserve energy and rations.
- We are by water.
- We have shelter.
- Liew [one of the Hong Kong soldiers] said helicopters available.
- We can be seen from the air.
- This is the most suitable spot in this part of the gully for a helicopter to get in.

Their team was already two days late for their return to headquarters, and they hoped this would alert the Malaysians to begin a search for them. On March 7, the weather finally cleared, and Neill and Foster began gathering slate-gray rocks to form a giant "SOS" on the mossy green surface of the gully. Foster also made the number "5" out of stones to indicate there were five people in need of help. Along with the stones, they laid out pieces of aluminum to reflect light and a red equipment bag to attract any rescuers' eyes.

Caves can sometimes make good shelters.

In the meantime, Neill pondered the fate of the other five-man team. He wondered where they had gone and how they had been separated. He felt intense guilt for getting his men into this life-threatening situation. One of his biggest concerns, of course, was rations: they had to be given out each day in smaller and smaller portions. Soon they would be gone completely. And without food, would the men be strong enough to climb out of the gully themselves, if it came down to that?

On March 11, Neill and Foster departed from the cave in order to look for a way out. The two officers, along with the rest of the men, were in bad physical shape. But they needed to do something. Very quickly, however, Neill and Foster realized how difficult it was to cut through the jungle lining the gully's walls. It was harder still to climb the steep embankments, and eventually they came to the end of their efforts when they faced a totally vertical wall of mud and loose stone. Both admitted defeat.

The next morning, however, brought hope when they were awoken by the sound of a helicopter. They immediately scrambled to signal it, Foster rapidly firing the flash of his camera and both laying out any reflective equipment they had on the ground. They returned to the cave with **optimism**, but after several days of waiting, they realized the helicopter had not seen them. Help was not on its way.

optimism: a belief that good things will come.

Back at the cave, conditions were worsening. The men were slowly starving. The only nutrition they had left was salt and sugar supplements, and a few **glucose** tablets. Their clothes and bedding were wet and rotting, providing less shelter and exposing them to more disease by the day.

glucose: a sugar; the body's main energy source.

On Saturday, March 19, Foster made a decision to go out on his own for one last attempt to escape. Foster was bigger and heavier built than the rest of the men. He made preparations for the worst, asking the men to write down on pieces of paper their wills and last wishes.

He set out on March 20, and his desperation pushed him up an incredible 70-degree slope. Struggling through thick vegetation and using dangerous footholds, Foster used up the last of his strength while still some hundred feet below the gully's ridge. That night he fell into an exhausted sleep.

The next morning, he awoke feeling helpless. But then he heard the unexpected sound of a helicopter. This time the helicopter remained for a longer period of time, but again it took off and disappeared. Defeated, Foster returned to the cave.

The next few nights were the darkest yet. The smell of rotting boots and clothes filled the air. Neill noticed his urine had now turned from dark yellow to an even darker brown. Clean water was scarce, and both disease and dehydration were looming. The officers wrote that every man felt as if the gully were closing in on them, eating them alive.

Then on Friday, March 25, the thirtieth day in the gully, a helicopter arrived and hovered directly above their camp. There was no mistaking it this time: the people in the helicopter had seen them! As if from heaven, a bag of rations with a note tied to it dropped from the helicopter . . . only to land in a pool of water. They were able to salvage the food, though, but only part of the note was still legible: "HELP IS ON ITS WAY. ENCLOSED ARE RATIONS. HANG ON IN THERE LADS."

The men had been saved. Soon after, the entire party, including the missing team members, was lifted out of the cave and taken to safety. They were fortunate to be alive.

Any kind of terrain or climate has its own survival challenges.

Chapter Four

LOST IN THE WOODS

For many of us, getting lost in the woods may be an experience we've already had. It's common for children to explore the land around them, and there is a certain mystery to be solved in the dark woods around your home. Even during the day, a thick wood can block out sunlight and seem like an entirely different world, full of surprises and adventure.

But getting lost in the woods isn't always so harmless. In fact, because woodlands make up so much of the **temperate zones** in our world, it's most likely that if you were to get lost *somewhere*, it would be in the woods. Even when help is only a few miles away, people have died walking in circles, retracing their footsteps.

In his *Outdoor Survival Book*, the EMT William Keller recounts a rescue operation he participated in to find a lost hunter. It was winter,

temperate zones: the part of the world between the tropical regions and the polar regions, having less extremes in temperature.

and that made the operation urgent. The missing hunter had not returned to camp as planned. Keller's role in the search was to be a "spotter" on the rescue helicopter. Along with the pilot, he scanned the snow-covered ground for any signs of the hunter's tracks. About two miles away from camp, they found them. They began tracking the hunter by flying directly over those tracks, imagining the hunter's condition by the story the tracks left behind.

The tracks looked good at first. They were normal and evenly spaced and, even better, they stopped after a mile and a pile of yellow snow appeared. This meant the man was remaining calm and was hydrated enough to urinate. Both good signs.

At about the three-and-a-half–mile point, Keller and his pilot noticed the stride length become more uneven. The tracks became less direct from point to point, and more looping. Sometimes the tracks even stopped and doubled back over themselves—evidence the hunter was second-guessing himself. It appeared he was getting more desperate.

At the four-mile point, the tracks were extremely uneven. They could see he was exhausted, probably dehydrated, and no longer at all certain of his path. His footprints changed, revealing he had switched from a normal step to one that favored his heel, which is usually a sign of numb or frozen toes. He began using his rifle as a walking stick, another sign that he had begun to get desperate. A hunter would not risk ruining his best tool by using it as a walking stick unless he was very tired.

At the five-mile mark, they observed gear that had been discarded by the hunter. This is an indicator of hypothermia. Often hypothermia victims begin to feel burdened by gear, feeling it abnormally heavy, and throw it off in a panic. The rescuers noticed, however, that the gear left behind was selected carefully, giving them hope that the man was still thinking clearly. As confirmation of this, shortly after they spotted the gear they also

When you're lost in the woods, it's easy to get turned around, and landmarks can blend together.

The woods can be very dark at night, and even familiar areas can look unfamiliar.

spotted a place where the man had sat down to rest, and begun using a walking stick instead of his rifle.

In later interviews with the man, he said that it was at this point he had begun to take mental hold of himself and think through his situation. At the seven-mile point, the rescuers began to realize the man was heading towards a vantage point from which to see his surroundings. This too showed he was still rational. His effort, however, was exhausted as he realized he could not physically push himself to a high enough altitude. In an open area visible by air he tramped the word "HELP" in large letters, with an arrow pointing toward where he was headed. They continued to follow.

At the seven-and-one-half–mile point, it seemed the hypothermia had taken over, and he had tossed his rifle into the snow. His course again became irrational. But the rescuers were very near now. They caught up to him at the eight-mile mark, exhausted and nearly unconscious. He had frostbite on his hands and feet. He had spent two nights outside. The rescue team saved his life, but he lost all toes on one foot, three toes on the other foot, and three fingers to frostbite.

TWO MEN, TWO STORIES OF SURVIVAL

Survival in woodland areas is often greatly determined by how the person maintains control of his emotions. William Keller tells the following two stories of men in woodland areas who reacted in very different ways to their situations.

The first man was in his early fifties. He was reported missing after he failed to return on time from a hunting trip into a wilderness area. A winter storm had turned into a two-day blizzard, trapping and severely **disorienting** the man. Friends of the man described to

disorienting: confusing; causing one to lose one's sense of location.

diabetic: having diabetes, a disorder caused by insufficient amounts or use of insulin creating high levels of glucose in the blood and causing severe thirst and high-urine output.

him to the rescuers as five feet, four inches (1.6 m), weighing 300 pounds (135 kg). He was a **diabetic** with high blood pressure. In general, this was not a very physically healthy man. To make matters worse, the man was wearing very little protective clothing—mostly cotton, which is very ineffective in wet conditions such as the ones he was experiencing in the blizzard. All signs pointed to a deadly outcome.

The blizzard was intense, and the search rescue had to wait until it cleared enough to put a few rescue helicopters in the air. By this time, the hunter had been trapped in the storm for over 72 hours. When the helicopter began tracking the hunter, it was only five minutes before he emerged from the trees, waving his hands at the rescuers. He had no injuries and no hypothermia. He was healthy. The rescuer, Keller, got out of the helicopter so the man could be lifted to safety more quickly (fewer persons in a helicopter allow it to fly at higher altitudes.) While waiting for another pickup, Keller decided to check out the man's camp.

What he found was amazing. When the man realized a storm was coming, he'd quickly stopped walking and built a shelter for himself. He'd stumbled upon an old elk-hunter shelter in the trees where a few scraps of trash and an empty whiskey bottle lay, and he'd used what he found to build a fire and a lean-to shelter against one of the trees. He had then used the whiskey bottle

as a container for snow that he melted beside the fire. With the exception of a few cold nights, the man had managed to avoid any emergency medical situations for three days in the wild.

Tree branches or driftwood can be used to create a makeshift shelter.

The second incident occurred that same day. A lost cross-country skier was reported. The man was described as in excellent health, in his late twenties, very healthy, and wearing weather-appropriate gear. Best of all, the storm had passed, and the weather was now much warmer. As Keller tells it, he and his team would normally had given the skier a few hours to come in on his own, but because the helicopter was already fueled, they left immediately.

Only thirty minutes into the search, the rescuers in the helicopter spotted the skier's tracks and began looking for the man, assuming they'd find him in moderate good health. In reality, had the rescue team not left when they did, the man would have perished. As they tracked the man, they realized he was in serious trouble. His tracks had all the characteristics of hypothermia and panic: a **nonsensical** path, with clothes, jackets, and skis thrown to the sides. Hypothermia victims suffer hallucinations and often feel suffocated under their clothing, causing them to panic and make **irrational** choices. When rescuers found the man, he was wearing only his shoes and snow pants. He would have died within two hours had the team not found him. He had been lost only a few hours.

nonsensical: meaningless, without sense.

irrational: without reason.

Tents are good shelters, even in the snow.

The contrast between the cases is obvious. One man kept a level head and used his experience to guide him through rational decisions. The other lost track of his emotions and panicked.

What's the application here for the rest of us, those of us who aren't out in the woods but are merely trying to make it through daily life? We'll do better if we don't panic, no matter how serious the situation. Our mental abilities are an important survival tool—whether we're surviving a night alone in the woods, or the challenges of an ordinary day.

TAKE YOUR TIME, BUILD A FIRE

The first thing you must do when you realize you are lost is stop. Don't waste valuable time and energy before you've thought

An example of what a hiker might take in his backpack. Along with extra clothes, a compass, bug spray, and water purification tablets are a few of the things included.

about where you are. There's no point getting yourself more lost, and more tired out in the process!

Once you realize you're lost, begin to mentally retrace your steps back to familiar territory. You must stay calm to accomplish this. Panic will only make it harder to concentrate. While resting, you not only save yourself energy you may need to survive in the wild, but you also help yourself stay positive. You can remind yourself that being lost is not the end of the world; laugh at yourself, and envision positive outcomes to this experience.

This resting place, where you plan your next move, is also ideal for building a fire.

Building a fire is key to survival, as it gives you both physical and emotional support. While keeping you warm and providing a way to boil water and cook food, fire also gives you a task to do—it keeps you busy. It keeps your mind on a **productive** activity. And it serves as a companion as well. A fire can also be your ticket to getting rescued.

productive: capable of bringing about a result.

THE FIRST NIGHT ALONE

Wilderness survival experts have what they call the "Four-o'Clock Rule." It's pretty simple: if it's after 4 p.m. and you're lost, you only have a few hours of sunlight left, so make plans to spend the night alone.

Fire is your first priority, so be sure to gather enough fuel to keep it going all night if necessary. Once you have what you think is enough, gather more, since you do not want to be wandering in the dark if you run out. Also gather wet, green materials to put on the fire in case you need to signal to rescuers overhead. These materials produce smoke, and pine needles and dry leaves make the fire itself flare up. Gather samples of both if possible.

Your next priority is finding or building a shelter. The type of shelter will of course depend on where you are lost and the time of year. If it's summertime and fairly warm, then you may not need much more than a lean-to, a simple shelter built of sticks leaned against a tree and covered in leaves and soil.

The Big Dipper is the easiest constellation to locate.

Also, remember that even if it is summertime, the nights can be significantly colder than days. Although it may not feel like you need a shelter for the night, build one anyway, as it can be useful for protection from rain too. And if it is wintertime, then you will need

Finding the North Star

The stars are some of the best navigation tools available to a lost person—but they won't do you any good if you don't know how to read them.

The key to locating the North Star in the night sky is to first find the Big Dipper, probably the best-known group of stars in the northern sky. Also known as the Great Bear (or Ursa Major), the Big Dipper is located just north of the celestial pole. Knowing how to find the Big Dipper makes it easy to find the North Star.

The second key to finding the North Star is a similarly shaped constellation of stars known as the Little Dipper, or the Little Bear (Ursa Minor), a smaller and less obvious group of stars. Fortunately its big brother the Big Dipper points the way. Locate the two stars that form the outer edge of the Big Dipper. Draw an imaginary line straight through the two stars of the dipper edge and toward the Little Dipper. The line will point very close to the handle of the Little Dipper. The brightest star in the Little Dipper is at the end of its handle. This is the North Star.

to put a lot more effort into finding someplace warm and dry. A shelter well under a fir or pine tree can be a good choice, as both naturally provide cover from rain and snow. Survey the area for rock, tree, and snow formations that might naturally provide good shelter. Then look for leaves, pine boughs, or anything that will make a good liner for your shelter's bedding, walls, and ceiling.

When darkness finally does come, your job isn't over. If the night is clear, and you can see the stars, use them to locate yourself. Spotting the North Star allows you mark directions for the next day.

When morning arrives, you have more decisions to make. If anyone knows your destination or approximate location, you should stay put and be ready to signal for help with your fire. If you have provisions (food, water, materials to start another fire), then you may want to consider traveling. If you do decide to travel, be sure to leave something at your campsite indicating where you went. If possible, leave a note for ground rescuers. For help from the sky, use pine boughs to make an arrow pointing out your direction, or tramp out an arrow in the snow.

ON THE MOVE

If you know the direction you were originally walking before you get lost, then keep track of your new direction. If you know the sun is rising in the east and setting in the west, then that too can help you determine which way you're walking. But even besides these basic techniques, observe landmarks wherever you go. If you have the materials available, you can tie markers around trees and shrubs in order to help rescuers track you.

At night, look for lights in the distance. Even from very far away, radio towers and the soft glow of city lights can be seen. Try to carry

A man signals with a hand mirror.

many different navigational tools when you travel in the woods. Learn how to use these tools and don't rely on just one. Global Positioning Systems (or GPS) are wonderful tools and easy to use, but can be easily damaged by rain or cold. Knowing how to properly use a map and compass is an invaluable skill.

Being on the move doesn't mean you can't be looking for food and other valuable resources along the way. Part of an effective survivor mentality is keeping a wide focus for anything that could aid your journey.

Tents are easy to use and lightweight.

SurvivalTopics.com gives the following explanation for "on-the-go foraging":

1. You are attempting to walk from point A to point B, perhaps toward help.

2. The wild foods you gather should be on the direct route of travel and require a minimum of time and effort for **acquisition**.

acquisition: the act of acquiring or getting something.

3. You do not veer off your chosen path to chase after anything fleeing,

and thereby use up precious energy and time that may become wasted effort.

4. You throw away any food prejudices you may have. Remember, insects and other creepy crawlies are being used as food on a daily basis by many cultures throughout the world. Do not put your survival at risk due to ignorance.

The idea for successful survival foraging is to keep a constant eye out for easy-to-get wild edibles no matter how small or of what type (animal, insect, or plant) they might be. Stick to your route and pause momentarily to collect edibles of opportunity as you go. This means that anything you harvest is almost free energy since you have to walk the route anyway and you will need occasional rest breaks that the collection of food will conveniently provide.

HELP THEM FIND YOU

Before even going out into the woods, taking a few steps can make yourself easier to find if you get lost.

First of all, wear bright clothing, or any color that will contrast with your surroundings. Even hunters should keep brightly colored garments beneath their camouflage. Think a great deal about visibility. Even a bright hat could make it easier to find you.

Carry matches and tinder. As discussed earlier, fire is one of your best allies to being rescued. Smoke rising out of trees is unnatural (so it calls attention to itself) and can be seen from miles away. If there is little wind, a single campfire can create a massive smoke plume. Again, pine needles and other green materials will create the most smoke. At night, a fire is easy to spot; the smoke may not be visible, but light from the fire illuminates the surrounding trees. Keep materials nearby for stoking your fire if you hear a plane or helicopter overhead.

Sound detection is as important as visual detection. If you're hunting or have a firearm of some kind with you, the standard help signal is three shots fired in quick succession. Many hunters carry a small pistol for this purpose, as this sound is distinct from a rifle and will be particularly alarming to anyone looking for you. Also consider firing shots at night, when no one is hunting, so the message will be clearer. Whistles are another kind of valuable tool in wilderness survival; you can sustain the noise for a longer period of time without exhausting yourself, whereas yelling and screaming will only wear you down. Save verbal contact for when you can actually hear rescuers nearby.

One final tool to consider bringing with you on any treks into the woods is the signal mirror. This can be any mirror small enough to fit in a pocket or backpack. It needn't be large or magnified. The basic goal is to reflect light from the sun into a faraway rescuer's field of vision. William Keller, EMT, says that it's surprising how well helicopter rescue teams can spot these mirror signals. Even in a dense forest, where the lost person might be almost totally hidden from sight, they are able to signal for help.

SLEEPING SURVIVAL

Sometimes the best thing you can do is nothing at all. Take a look at the following advice from survival experts at SurvivalTopics.com:

> As expert survivors we often think in terms of taking action in order to survive. For example we have our bug-out bags pre-packed and ready to go, so that we may walk or drive many miles with enough supplies to get us there. Survivors know how to build a fire in many different ways under a variety of adverse conditions. Survivors can obtain drinkable water and forage edible foods from a plethora of sources. As survival experts we can defend ourselves and our property to the best of our ability.
>
> And that is just the beginning. When the going gets tough the experienced wilderness and urban survivor springs into action, taking adversity head on.
>
> But not always. A wise old friend of mine once told me, "Sometimes the best thing you can do—is do nothing!"

When the conditions make it difficult to find one's way, for example in fog, it is often better to stay where you are.

When the going gets tough, sometimes the best thing to do is to take a long nap. Rather than flail about in wind and storm, simply go to sleep and wait it out! You will save your energy, reduce the risk of injury, and get a good rest besides.

This strategy has been employed by experienced wilderness survivors such as the northern Native Americans, arctic explorers, and high mountain expeditions like those on Mount Everest and K2. Even the squirrels and bears, nature's experienced survival instructors, will hunker down during the worst of conditions. They simply curl up in their dens and go to sleep.

During a survival situation of any kind, the ability to sleep warm, dry, and comfortable is very important and can mean the difference between health and the ability to take action during waking hours or possibly not making it out alive. If you have the proper survival gear and knowledge, your outdoor sleep system can get you through the most trying of times with little expenditure of precious energy or exposure to danger.

In order to take survival naps in adverse conditions you need to know a few things. Depending upon conditions you may need a portable shelter or know how to make a survival shelter with the materials you have at hand. A good sleeping bag is also handy, but you can often make your own sleeping bag using natural materials.

You might want to try this technique out in daily life as well. Sometimes just getting a good night's sleep can make all the difference in our ability to handle life's challenges!

Chapter Five

STAYING HEALTHY IN THE WILDERNESS

W e've already said that your mind is probably your most important survival tool. But your mind can't function well if your body isn't healthy. Meeting your body's needs is vital to survival in any wilderness situation.

FINDING WATER

Water is essential to life. In any and all survival situations in the wild, without water you will not last long. No matter how physically fit, no matter how much gear you have, without water you can last only three or four days at most.

Often wilderness survivors will focus only on rescue, an understandable response, but not a wise one. It's the "details" like thirst that will kill you. You might spend all day building signal fires and planning routes to civilization,

Finding water in the wilderness can mean the difference between life and death.

but slowly and steadily your thirst will take over until you're incapable of thinking of anything else. So whenever you're walking or hiking in the wild, take careful note of any water sources. Streams, ponds, lakes, and creeks—all could be useful to you in a survival situation.

Dehydration and Heat Exhaustion

Having enough water in your system is important for many reasons, and one of them is avoiding heat exhaustion. Without water, the body really can't perform any of its major heat-releasing processes. Perspiration becomes impossible with insufficient fluids. So does proper circulation, which normally would allow the heart to redistribute heat throughout the body. As the body overheats, you will become increasingly dizzy and weak. This can be very dangerous if you're on your own in the wild. If you continue on without water, you may become unconscious. Luckily, if fluids are restored, you can recover very quickly—as soon as thirty minutes. Just remember that **heat stroke** is a possibility in temperate and cold-weather climates as much as it is in hot ones. Whenever you physically exert yourself without proper hydration, you take some risk of overheating.

heat stroke: a serious condition in which the body's ability to regulate its temperature is impaired, causing headache, fever, lack of sweating, and, if untreated, collapse, coma, or even death.

Water from Snow

Contrary to what you might think, getting water from snow is not always as simple as eating one cold handful at a time. In fact, doing so can sometimes be deadly. First of all, if you're forced to **ingest** snow for water then likely you're already in a survival situation and have a low body temperature. Ingesting snow will only cause your internal temperature to sink lower, and it can contribute to hypothermia.

Second, snow is not always clean. Freshly fallen snow is cleaner than old snow, and you should look for it. Avoid anything with a pink or yellowish tint. Once you've found

ingest: to take into the body; eat.

clean snow, you should melt it if at all possible. If you have a water bottle or container to hold the snow, but no way to start a fire, then fill the bottle with snow and place it between layers of your clothing. Avoid direct contact with your skin, which could drastically reduce your body temperature. Once half the bottle has melted, shake the remaining mixture. This uses the existing water to help melt the ice. You can repeat this process once the entire contents have melted, never drinking past the halfway point before filling the second half of the bottle with snow again, then shaking and repeating the process.

Finding Other Water Sources

Being able to find water in the wilderness is one of the most useful skills you can have. It takes a great deal of time and experience to recognize the variety of different water sources.

Lesson one is to always look for water drainage: where is the water flowing? Usually this means following rainwater down hill until you find a creek, a stream, or some other water source. Also remember to not miss the obvious: if you see domestic animals nearby, then probably there are water tanks or some natural water source. If you have a dog with you, set him loose and see where he goes. Often dogs are able to smell water from great distances. Other animals are useful for this too, including wild animals: animal paths usually **converge** near a water source

converge:
come together.

of some kind, so if you follow them long enough, you may find a water source. Don't forget about vegetation either. Dark green leaves and thick vegetation are an excellent sign that water is near. Last, keep your eyes to the sky: birds tend to head toward water in the early morning and just before dark. Waterfowl will sometimes circle above water during the day.

Snow can be melted for drinking water, and pine needles can be boiled or eaten raw.

Water Sources

Most people think that springs offer the best and purest water, but unfortunately, not all spring water is of equal quality. First of all, not everything that appears to be spring water really is spring water. Sometimes what looks like spring water is actually just the overflow from another water source. But if the water is, in fact, from a spring, it is just as likely to be exposed to pollutants as any other water source. Very few springs have naturally pure water anymore. Be sure to take necessary steps to purify spring water.

Other natural water sources—lakes, rivers, creeks, and ponds—should be approached with similar levels of caution. A good rule to remember: clear water is not necessarily safe water. Just because a water sample looks clean and transparent does not mean it is free of bacteria and other invisible pollutants. On the other hand, not all cloudy water is harmful. Cloudiness is caused by particulates (little bits of floating material), some of which are safer than others.

Purifying Water

Boiling is usually the first method people think of when they consider purifying water, but it is actually much more difficult than you might think. The problem is that water must boil for ten minutes in order to kill most impurities. Unless you have a relatively large container for boiling, you won't have much water left after you're done. Most wilderness experts advise you to treat boiling as a secondary means of water purification. Methods that are quicker and easier to carry are available. However, if you do have the means to boil water, then do so. Save your backup options for a time when you might not be able to build a fire.

Iodine pills offer one of those alternative methods that is cheap and effective. One small bottle of pills can treat a large amount of water. Simply drop the pills into your water source, two to three pills (or drops) of iodine for every two pints of water (about 1 liter), then let it sit for about thirty minutes. Be sure to clean the rim of your water container to remove any raw iodine trapped there.

Filters are one of the best ways to purify water. They come in many shapes and sizes, but the basic concept is the same: pass water through a screen with tiny pores, allowing only pure water (or nearly pure water, depending on the filter) to pass through.

Mushrooms should usually be avoided in the wild, since there are so many similar-looking varieties, not all of them edible.

Straw filters are the smallest of the filtration systems. They are exactly what they sound like, straws with filters in them. Their flaw is they cannot purify a container of water for cooking or other purposes, but they can make safe whatever you drink. They are extremely light and easy to carry.

Also popular and very effective are water pumps. These pumps vary in size and capacity, and operate using two hoses and one filter. They pump water out of a water source, through a filter, and into your container. EMT William Keller recommends such water pumps as your primary means of water filtration, but insists that other means should be brought along—as many as three or four systems, if possible. Although it seems like a lot to carry, clean water is a number-one **priority** in the wild.

priority: rank determining order of importance.

monitor: to watch closely and observe.

Some berries are poisonous and some are edible, but it can be difficult to determine which is which.

FOOD IN THE WILD

You can't eat everything you find in the wilderness. Something that looks like food—juicy red berries, for instance—could actually be poison. You must constantly **monitor** yourself and be careful not to let your hunger drive you to eat something without knowing what it is. The truth is the human body can actually survive for weeks without food. So as much as your stomach might complain, keep that in mind in a survival situation.

Some people have dietary requirements outside the norm for humans. This includes diabetics or those with digestive disorders. If you fall into this category, don't despair—wilderness training and survival is still possible. Simply make more preparations to ensure your safety. When taking trips, pack enough food for three or four days if you only plan on being gone for one. Always allot yourself more food than you think you'll need.

Grasshoppers and other insects can be eaten if necessary.

Another important rule is to always second guess plants and berries. For almost every edible plant in the wild there is a poisonous or harmful variety that looks nearly the same. In general, unless you have intimate knowledge of the local plants, avoid eating them altogether.

A Warning

Although descriptions of plants and berries are helpful, there is no substitute for someone native to the land who can tell you personally what is safe and what is not. For further reading on foraging in the wild for food, consult a book with extensive color photos that is dedicated

What You Can and Can't Eat in the Wilderness

Plants to Avoid
- mushrooms (some are edible, but unless you are 100 percent certain, don't eat one)
- umbrella-shaped flower clusters
- plants with a milky or black sap
- bulbs
- carrot-like leaves, roots, or tubers
- bean or pea-like appearance
- shiny leaves or those with fine hairs
- white, yellow, and green berries

Edible Plants
- grass: Stems, roots, and leaves are edible (don't eat black or purple grass leaves).
- cattails: In spring, the young shoots and flower heads are the most edible portions and can be peeled and eaten raw or boiled. During the summer, the flower's pollen can be eaten raw.
- pine trees with sharp needles arranged in bundles of 2, 3, or 5. Pine needles may be eaten raw or cooked. Boiled in water they make tea. The layer between the bark and inner wood can be eaten raw or cooked. The seeds, located under the scales of the cones, may be eaten raw or cooked.
- common green seaweed: Seaweed on shore is probably rotten; instead, gather it off rocks or directly from the sea.
- dandelions: The entire plant is edible; leaves and buds are the best.
- chickweed: This plant grows throughout North America; the leaves are dandelion-like; flowers are light blue. The leaves and roots are edible.
- crabapple: The small, tart fruit can be eaten raw or boiled.
- watercress: This surface water plant thrives wild throughout much of North America; it's sometimes seen growing in a luxuriant green mat overflowing a shallow trough at the edge of a slow-running stream.
- purple, blue, and black berries are usually edible.

(*Source:* William Keller's *Outdoor Survival Guide*)

to the plant life of a particular region. This is the surest way to learn more safely.

INJURIES IN THE WILD

Building fires and signaling for rescue can do little to help you or your companions if one of you is injured. That's why experts suggest you always travel in the wilderness with a well-prepared first-aid kit. William Keller suggests the following "basic kit":

- adhesive bandages of varying sizes to keep small cuts clean and to cover blisters

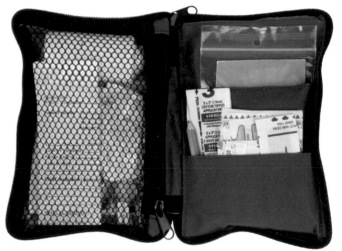

- sterile gauze dressing and gauze bandages for larger wounds and burns
- elastic bandage for sprains or for keeping limbs immobilized
- ibuprofen or aspirin for swelling and pain relief
- antiseptic cream or ointment
- antiseptic wipes
- a small pair of quality scissors
- safety pins
- corn pads and foot felt for blisters and other foot problems

It's always a good idea to take a first-aid kit with you while hiking.

- a large square bandage that can be used as a sling or to bandage a wound

Snakebites

The Western Diamondback Rattlesnake is one of many species of rattlesnake found in North America.

Snakes are really not the widespread killers that some of us think they are. In the United States annually, only fifteen of the 40,000 reported snakebite cases are fatal. In fact, the snakes we most commonly interact with are nonpoisonous. Still, a good rule to follow is to stay out of a snake's way. Snakes are easily frightened and will do anything to get away from danger. If you uncover a snake under a rock or log, do not panic, but rather give the snake room to escape. Getting in its way will only threaten it. It's important to stay calm.

There are two breeds of poisonous snake in the United States: the pit viper snakes

(including rattlesnakes, water moccasins, and copperheads) and the coral snake. If one of these snakes does bite you: again, stay calm! Even these snakes are usually unable to inject a fatal dose of poison into your body.

First, try to get a good look at what kind of snake it is. This information will help your rescuers select the correct anti-venom to save your life. The more excited you are, the faster your heart beats, and the faster your blood will carry the venom through your system. So a third time: stay calm! Get help as soon as possible. If someone you're traveling with is bitten, follow these simple guidelines from Keller:

- Stay calm and keep the patient lying down. The quieter you stay, the less you will spread the poison through the blood system.
- Clean the wound with soap and **copious** amounts of water. The use of an antiseptic will help prevent infection.
- Place a restriction above the bitten area—a constrictive band, belt, or other restriction that resembles a tourniquet around the limb. Unlike a tourniquet, this is not intended to shut down arterial circulation. You want to slow the **venous circulation**, which will carry the poison back into the body, but you do not want to interfere with deeper **arterial circulation**. After application of the

copious: plentiful.

venous circulation: the movement of blood through veins, the blood vessels carrying blood toward the heart.

arterial circulation: the movement of blood through arteries, the blood vessels carrying blood away from the heart and throughout the body.

Copperheads are another variety of poisonous snakes found in North America.

shock: *a serious medical condition in which not enough blood is circulated throughout the body. It can be brought on by a number of external or internal factors, such as major injury and blood loss, infections, or toxins.*

aspiration: *breathing liquid or foreign matter into the lungs.*

restriction, you should be able to feel a pulse in the extremity below the bite.

- Splint the bitten limb to prevent movement. Watch the victim carefully, monitoring the vital signs.
- Elevate the legs, treating for **shock** and keeping the patient warm.
- Transport the patient as soon as possible.
- Do not allow the patient to eat.
- Be careful if the patient vomits. **Aspiration** of vomit is as much a threat as is the poison. It is common for a patient to vomit as a result of anxiety or fear of dying, and not because of the poison.
- Do not give the patient any alcohol.

"REAL-LIFE" LESSONS

Obviously, you may never be in a wilderness survival situation. So what's the lesson you can take away from all this?

No matter what challenges you face in life—whether you're "surviving" finals' week or you're lost in the woods—you'll do better if you take care of your body. Drink plenty of water, eat carefully and healthfully, and do your best to care for any injuries or illnesses. None of us are at our best if we're not well.

When you were a little kid, it was your parents' or guardians' job to take care of your physical needs. As you get older, that changes. Now it's your responsibility!

Snake bites need to be treated as soon as possible, or they can cause permanent damage.

Chapter Six

WHAT DOES IT TAKE TO SURVIVE?

In today's world, people seem to expect they should have a sense of security wherever they go—at least physical security. Most people are confident that when they step out of their house in the morning, their immediate health will not be threatened. Food, water, and shelter are all within a phone call (or a click of a mouse). Even remote locations are more safely accessed with the increasing effectiveness of communication technologies. A person lost in dense woods might only need to find a high enough point for cell-phone reception!

Despite this, survival skills are just as necessary today, if not more so than ever before. When life-or-death scenarios do arise in our world, possessing those skills may make you the one and only person who can take proper action. Are you prepared? William Keller encourages us to ask ourselves the following questions when answering this question:

- If you became lost or stranded, what would you do?
- If you were driving your car and the engine quit on a remote road, it was cold, and the heater no longer worked, what would you do?
- If you were lost, getting thirsty, and did not have any drinking water, would you know how to find a safe drink of water?
- Can you build a shelter to protect yourself from the elements?
- Can you build a fire?
- Can you build a fire in windy or wet conditions?
- Can you build a fire when your hands are cold and numb—so numb that you cannot hold a match or lighter?
- Do you know how to dry your clothing after a rain or if you have fallen into a stream?
- Would you recognize the symptoms of hypothermia in yourself or someone else before it was too late?
- Do you know how to warm yourself or a companion who is in a condition of hypothermia without causing further dangers, such as cardiac arrest?
- Do you know what you can and cannot eat in the wild?

- Do you know how to dress yourself for the conditions you will be
  exposed to? Will those clothes work
  if the conditions change?
- If you have a GPS guidance system,
  what would you do if the batteries
  died or it was damaged and no longer worked?
- Do you have the ability to use a map
  and compass? Do you *have* a map
  and compass?
- Can you determine direction by the
  stars?

Ultimately, the best survival skills take the
form of preparation and experience. Reading

Do you
know what it
would take to
survive in any
environment?

books like this one are a great start. They arm you with good information. But if they never lead to real-life practice, then that information is useless. Even something as basic as building a fire requires years of practice to really achieve **proficiency**. And to be able to build a fire in the middle of a snowstorm—well, that takes a whole different level of practice and preparation.

proficiency:
skill and ability.

INSIDE THE MIND OF A SURVIVOR

As Laurence Gonzalez points out in *Deep Survival*, physical characteristics are actually a very small component of the survivor's whole. In fact, children under the age of six years old have done very well in certain survival situations. Women and children often fair better than men with bigger, stronger physiques. Body isn't everything in the wild. In fact, it can be very little when stripped of its necessities. Under these extreme conditions, the mind becomes more important than ever before. In fact, these were probably the very conditions where humans first learned to use their minds to exceed all other creatures in **adaptation**.

adaptation:
the process of changing to better fit the circumstances and environment.

POSITIVE THINKING

It has been said time and time again: keep a positive mental attitude. Included in this idea of a "positive attitude" is the equally important concept most commonly known

as "the will to live." Both can be rather vague concepts, and Laurence Gonzalez helpfully breaks them down into twelve "rules of survival." They are as follows:

- Perceive and believe.
- Stay calm—use your anger.
- Think, analyze, and plan.
- Take correct, decisive action.
- Celebrate your success.
- Be a rescuer, not a victim.
- Enjoy the survival journey.
- See the beauty.
- Believe that you will succeed.
- Surrender.
- Do whatever is necessary.
- Never give up.

Those who live close to nature sometimes develop wilderness survival skills as a necessity.

THE BASIC STRATEGY

Survival, says Gonzalez and other survival experts, should be thought of as a journey, not an isolated event. The best survivors have certain thought patterns and habits that follow them around wherever they go—whether they're in the office or the top of a snowy mountain.

Perceive and Believe

Admit your situation and be objective about your condition. You are really in trouble and you are really going to have to work hard to escape. The survival journey must begin as other psychological journeys begin—with acceptance. But acceptance is actually the last of a series of mental phases: denial, anger, bargaining, depression, and *finally*, acceptance. A survivor is the kind of person who can move steadily and quickly through these phases in order to get active.

Stay Calm—Use Your Anger as a Tool

Survivors are usually people who at some point or another in their survival experience were able to manage their emotions effectively. They turned their pain and emotional distress into a helpful motivation rather than let it rule them into submission. Aron Ralston, when he first realized his hand was caught between the rock and the ravine, thrashed violently in despair. But he quickly recovered. Throughout the next five days, Ralston had occasional outbursts of anger, but even these he scolded himself for, knowing they did him no good. Eventually, he was able to use his pent-up anger to break the bones in his arm and free himself from the ravine. He did not become a slave to his emotions, but rather made them work to his advantage.

Think, Analyze, and Plan

Not only do survivors submit their emotions to their will to survive, but they also actively cultivate a strong voice of reason. They form systems and make plans. They do not panic. They assess their **predicament** and make arrangements. While looking for help during the day, they are planning for the coming night. Instead of running through a snowstorm, they are building a shelter. All these things require a strong voice of reason. Gonzalez writes that survivors often report experiencing this as an almost audible "voice of reason."

predicament: a difficult or dangerous situation.

Take Correct, Decisive Action

Survivors do as much as they can as soon as they can, and no more or less. They do not attempt impossible acts of heroism, but do for others and themselves only what is possible in the present moment. They are present-minded when necessary, not allowing the looming future of doubt to cloud their vision. If a mountain needs to be descended, they will go from foothold to foothold. It may take

two days to complete, but each decision is concerned only with the next few minutes.

Celebrate Your Success

Survivors embrace the help that joy can be in times of hardship. If a small victory is won, they take the time to acknowledge it and let that success fuel their energy for the rest of the journey.

Be a Rescuer, Not a Victim

Survivors are often marked by compassion; in other words, they think about others, rather than focusing only on their own situation. They are the people who, even with a broken arm or fractured ribs, will try to assist others suffering. They are survivors not as an end goal, but as a product of their dedication to something or someone else.

When the pilot and author Antoine Saint-Exupery was stranded in the Libyan desert after his small plane crashed, he was carried through the experience by thinking of his wife and how she might suffer without him. Viktor Frankl, survivor of the Holocaust, says, "Don't aim at success—the more you aim at it and make it a target, the more you are going to miss it." Rather take success as "the unintended side-effect of one's personal dedication to a cause greater than oneself or as the by-product of one's surrender to a person other than oneself."

Enjoy the Survival Journey

If rescue becomes the only goal of the survival experience, and day after day goes by with no rescue, then a person will despair. But if this person begins to look around her, observing the complexity of the situation and the variety of life in her past and present, then time is passed more easily. Survivors who laugh at themselves and their predicament stand a much better chance of success. They stay as lighthearted as possible and do not disconnect themselves from their surroundings by wishing themselves away from the situation. They enjoy and participate in the experience as much as possible, and are safer for doing so.

See the Beauty

Saint-Exupery, trapped in the Libyan desert, found countless beauties in the ruins of his plane and the days spent looking for help. He savored even small beauties, for these were enormous treasures to him in his **impoverished** state. He wrote, "Here we are, condemned to death, and still the certainty of dying cannot compare with the pleasure I am feeling. The joy I take from this half an orange which I am holding in my hand is one of the greatest joys I have ever known."

impoverished: depleted, made poor or without strength or vitality.

Believe You Will Succeed

Survivors need to not only make a conscious decision to put away fears and doubts, but they must **actively** imagine a vision for how they will succeed. They paint a mental picture of their loved one's embrace, or the look on their friends' faces when they tell them the story of how they escaped.

actively: willingly and purposefully.

Surrender

Surrender for the survivor is not giving up the will to live. It is giving up the desire to be rescued or saved, while accepting—surrendering to—the immediate situation. It means giving yourself a positive goal rather than a negative one: replacing "don't die" with "keep moving, keep looking for an answer."

Do Whatever Is Necessary

Survivors take action according to what the situation calls for. They are not hindered by expectations but rather adapt themselves to the environment. They do not demand the situation they are in conform itself to their desires, but actively do whatever is necessary to answer the demands of the moment. This could mean eating an insect . . . or drinking their own urine . . . or even eating a dead human being. Survivors are willing to do whatever it takes.

Never Give Up

The lessons for everyday life are obvious—and in the end, they come down to this simple rule: never give up. Those who survive—whether it's gym class or a plane crash, soccer tryouts or a shipwreck, adapting to a new school or being lost in a desert—are those who keep moving, keep adapting: the ones who ultimately see opportunity in adversity rather than despair.

Our modern world bristles with technology, and the wilderness can seem far away and irrelevant. But nature is all around us, indifferent to our imposed boundaries. What does it mean to be human in the wilderness? To be human in situations that are dangerous or unfamiliar? Survival skills are great, but survival attitudes are better. No matter how small and weak you might feel in the midst of the wilderness—in the midst of any overwhelming and threatening circumstance—you are not helpless. And that is a very powerful attitude to have.

Further Reading

Connaughton, R. M. *Descent into Chaos: The Doomed Expedition to Low's Gully*. London, U.K.: Brassey's, 2006.

Davenport, Gregory J. *Wilderness Survival*. Mechanicsburg, Pa.: Stackpole Books, 1998.

Department of Defense. *US Army Survival Manual: FM 21-76*. BN Publishing, 2007.

Gonzalez, Laurence. *Deep Survival*. New York, N.Y.: W.W. Norton & Company, 2003.

Jamison, Richard and Linda Jamison (compilers). *Primitive Skills and Crafts: An Outdoorsman's Guide to Shelters, Tools, Weapons, Tracking, Survival, and More*. New York, N.Y.: Skyhorse Publishing, 2007.

McCullough, Jay. *The Ultimate Guide to U.S. Army Survival Skills, Tactics, and Techniques*. New York, N.Y.: Skyhorse Publishing, 2007.

Ralston, Aron. *Between a Rock and a Hard Place*. New York, N.Y.: Atria Books, 2004.

Wiseman, John Lofty. *SAS Survival Handbook: How to Survive in the Wild, in Any Climate, on Land or at Sea*. New York, N.Y.: Collins, 2004.

For More Information

Simple Survival
www.simpleSurvival.net
This veteran-operated site was created for the purpose of offering basic survival information to those who may encounter emergency survival situations, such as hunters, hikers, or campers.

Survival Gear Guide
www.survival-gear-guide.com/index.html
Includes not only helpful survival gear that would be useful to have on hand, but also basic survival information, and true stories of people who survived the wilderness.

SurvivalIQ
www.survivaliq.com
In-depth explanation of land navigation, cartography, survival fitness and nutrition, along with other basic survival information. Based partly on techniques used by the U.S. military, this guide could be imperative to surviving wilderness situations.

Survival Topics: Your Online Survival Kit!
www.survivaltopics.com
Contains a variety of topics with instructions and photographs explaining simply how to survive in different situations.

Survive Outdoors
www.surviveoutdoors.com
This Web site includes what to expect and how to take action when you encounter a variety of problems in the outside world, including sicknesses and wounds, along with various dangerous plants and animals.

For More Information

Wilderness Survival
www.wilderness-survival.net
Contains everything you need to know about how to survive in the wilderness, and how to prepare an adequate survival kit. Contains both quizzes and public forums, along with step-by-step instructions on what to do when stranded in the wild.

Wilderness Survival Skills for Safe Wilderness Travel
www.wilderness-survival-skills.com/index.
  html
This informative survival Web site includes thorough information on how to build fires and shelters, find food in the wilderness, create rescue signals, perform basic first aid, and many other necessary topics for those stranded in the wilderness.

Publisher's note:
The Web sites listed on this page were active at the time of publication. The publisher is not responsible for Web sites that have changed their addresses or discontinued operation since the date of publication. The publisher will review and update the Web-site list upon each reprint.

Benton, Gary L. "I Survived Three Days in the Arctic, and So Can You." www.simplesurvival. net/arctic.htm.

Curran, Jan D. *The Appalachian Trail*. Highland City, Fla.: Rainbow Books, 1995.

Gonzalez, Laurence. *Deep Survival*. New York, N.Y.: W.W. Norton & Company, 2003.

Keller, William. *Keller's Outdoor Survival Guide: How to Prevail When Lost, Stranded, or Injured in the Wilderness*. Minocqua, Wisc.: Willow Creek Press, 2001.

Knap, Jerome J. *The Complete Outdoorsman's Handbook*. Toronto, Ont.: Pagurian Press Limited, 1974.

Krakauer, Jon. *Into Thin Air*. New York, N.Y.: Villard, 1997.

Masters, Anthony. *Survival: True Stories of Human Perseverance and Courage*. New York, N.Y.: Galahad Books, 1997.

Middleton, Nick. *Extremes: Surviving the World's Harshest Environments*. New York, N.Y.: St. Martin's Press, 2005.

Olsen, Larry Dean. *Outdoor Survival Skills*, 6th edition. Chicago, Ill.: Chicago Review Press, 2000.

Ralston, Aron. *Between a Rock and a Hard Place*. New York, N.Y.: Atria Books, 2004.

Index

Picture Credits

CC a 2.0 Generic
  alka3en: p. 27
  Anderson Mancini: p. 103
  blacklord: p. 29
  bmarmie: p. 99
  Charles & Clint: p. 106
  Hamed Saber: p. 118
  Julius!: p. 109
  krossbow: p. 110
  Mat Honan: p. 82
  Matti Mattila: p. 18
  photogirl7: p. 12
  RickC: p. 20
  Steve Deger: p.68
  thomas_sly: p. 55
  winkyintheuk: p. 48
CC andw 2.0 Generic
  Bitterroot: p. 115
  Joel Bedford: p. 102
  jrwebbe: p. 64
  papalars: p. 34, 80
CC asa 2.0 Generic
  bogenfreund: p. 76
  hlkljgk: p. 108
  Ipoh: p. 14
  mariachily: p. 88

mattymatt: p. 40
pfly: p. 75
Pipiten: p. 57
ronnie44052: p. 36
s mestdagh: p. 52
Trinity: p. 79

DefenseImagery.mil
  MSGT Ed Boyce: p. 32
  CPL M. H. Coffey: p. 43
  MC2 Joshua J. Wah: p. 87

Jupiter Images: p. 30, 105

National Biological
Information Infrastructure
Public Domain.
  Randolph Femmer: p. 71, 96, 101
  John J. Mosesso: p. 11, 17, 92, 113

Wikimedia Commons
Public Domain.
  Gh5046: p. 84
  Oroval: p. 58, 62

To the best knowledge of the publisher, all images not specifically credited are in the public domain. If any image has been inadvertently uncredited, please notify Harding House Publishing Service, 220 Front Street, Vestal, New York 13850, so that credit can be given in future printings.

About the Author and the Consultant

Author

Zachary Chastain graduated from Wheaton College and currently lives in Endicott, New York, where he works as a writer and consultant.

Consultant

Andrew M. Kleiman, M.D. is a Clinical Instructor in Psychiatry at New York University School of Medicine. He received a BA in philosophy from the University of Michigan, and graduated from Tulane University School of Medicine. Dr. Kleiman completed his internship, residency, and fellowship in psychiatry at New York University and Bellevue Hospital. He is currently in private practice in Manhattan and teaches at New York University School of Medicine.